Conley

D1532863

If I Had
a Nickel...

Molly Schaar Idle

Abingdon Press

Nashville

If I Had a Nickel...

Copyright © 2005 by Abingdon Press
All rights reserved.

No part of this work may be reproduced or transmitted in any form
or by any means, electronic or mechanical, including photocopying and recording, or by any information storage
or retrieval system, except as may be expressly permitted by the 1976 Copyright Act
or by permission in writing from the publisher. Requests for permission should be submitted in writing to:
Abingdon Press, 201 Eighth Avenue South, Nashville, TN 37203;
faxed to (615) 749-6128; or submitted via email to *permissions@abingdonpress.com*.

Scripture quotation is from the New Revised Standard Version of the Bible.
Copyright © 1989 by the Division of Christian Education of the National Council of Churches of Christ in the U.S.A.
Used by permission.

Scripture quotation identified as NIV is from the HOLY BIBLE, NEW INTERNATIONAL VERSION.
Copyright © 1973, 1978, 1984 by International Bible Society.
Used by permission of Zondervan Publishing House. All rights reserved.

ISBN 0-687-32549-8

05 06 07 08 09 10 11 12 13 14—10 9 8 7 6 5 4 3 2 1

Printed in China

For D.

The light of my life.

"How priceless is your unfailing love!"
Psalm 36:7, NIV

If I had a nickel for every
special friend like you...

I'd have one brilliant nickel!

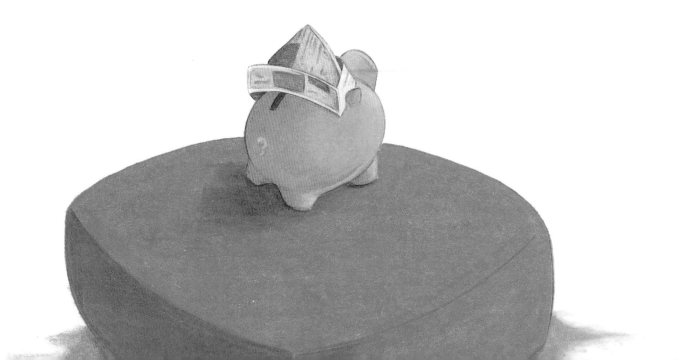

And...

If I had a nickel for every time
    you surprised me with delight...

I'd have a baker's dozen!

And...

If I had a nickel for every tear
    you've dried and turned to laughter...

My pockets couldn't hold them!

And...

If I had a nickel

for every day
    we've dreamed away...

I'd need a plethora of
piggy banks to keep them!

And...

If I had a nickel for every
hug and squeeze

and kiss...

I'd have bales full and bushels!

And...

If I had a nickel

for every happy memory...

They would fill up all the rivers
and spill into the sea.

And...

If I had a nickel for every time
I looked up to heaven
and
thanked God for you...

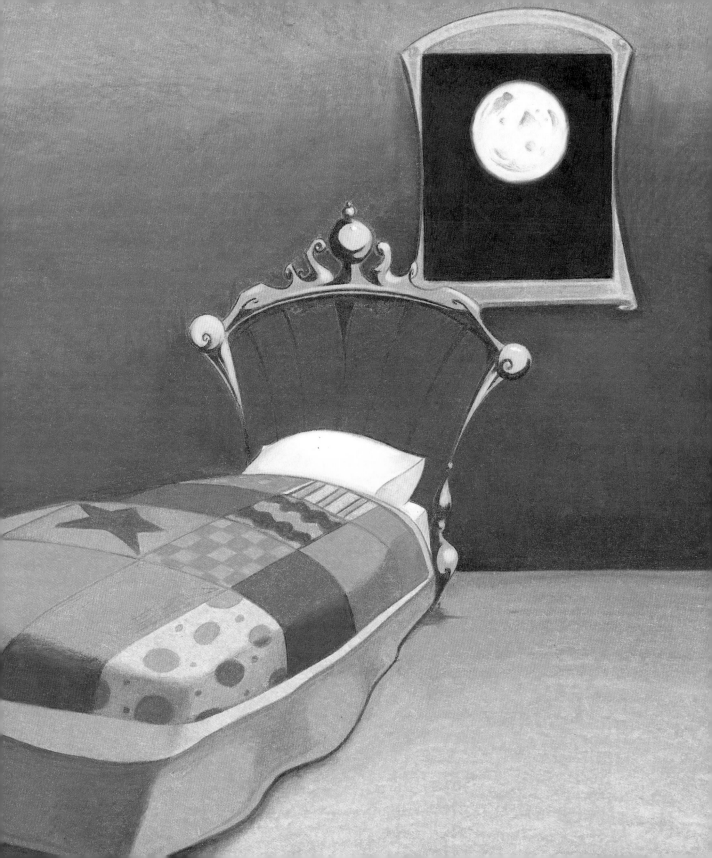

They would make a mountain
that would reach up to the moon!

But...

Even all those nickels
couldn't buy my love for you.

The End

"For this is the message you have heard
from the beginning,
that we should love one another."

1 John 3:11